D0764917

*twenty years*
*in bed*
*with the same man*

If you want to grow your heart
use the vowels from "man" and "woman."
Your heart will grow like a city
stretching out in spacious suburbs.
Your heart will be the color alba.
No more will you go on saying,
silencio and nada.

# TWENTY YEARS IN BED WITH THE SAME MAN

*Joan Logghe*

La ALAMEDA Press ◆ *Albuquerque*

## Acknowledgements

The following poems have appeared in these publications:

*Crosswinds:* "Heron Lake", "Loneliness", "Breakfast with John and Michael";
*FishDrum:* "The Middles", "Over and Over", "Reading in Bed";
*6 Poets of New Mexico / FishDrum Audio:* "The Homeless", "Icons", "Pavilion",
"The Russian Room";
*Hayden's Ferry Review:* "The Sugar Orchids";
*KIL~Culture, Art, Literature (a Bulgarian literary newspaper):* "After Reading
Love Lyrics From India", "The Lover" translated by *Bogomil Avramov;*
*Pittsburgh Post Gazette:* "Mixed Marriage";
*Puerto del Sol:* "Dawning on Your Birthday";
*Rhododendrun:* "Birch Bark Canoes", "You are Forty Years Old at the End of
the Twentieth Century, What Will You Do When Love Comes?";
*Sing Heavenly Muse!:* "Dream Is Quilt Is Comforter", "Wisconsin Blue Willow";
*The Taos Review:* "Dark Train Pulling";
*Yellow Silk Journal:* "I Don't Know Wide But I Know Deep", "Post Coital";
*Yoo Hoo Press;* "Dark Fiesta", "Conversations in Blue", "Snow Storm",
"Solid as Chocolate", "Exile" in the chapbook *THE DARK FACES OF LOVE*
with Miriam Sagan.

*With great appreciation to the National Endowment for the Arts,
whose support gave me time, space and faith.
¡Viva la NEA!*

Thank you Carolynne Colby-Schmeltzer and Renée Gregorio
of the farm team.

ISBN 0-9631909-7-0

La Alameda Press
9636 Guadalupe Trail NW
Albuquerque, New Mexico 87114

**for Michael**
**&**
*to all those*
*in it for the long haul*

## Table of Contents

*PART I*

# Taking Vows

## Mixed Marriage

My husband with no band, with a barb wire
voice and a closet full of verbs. My husband
of lapis lazuli. I gave my husband a power mower
for a wedding. Wed him under a hoopa
of evangelical hammers. I married him, a geisha
to a wok to a blue martin to a box of cornflakes.

I went to the church on a streetcar filled with
carnations. We ate carnations in public, man
and wildfire, husband and furnace. We tried to say
I do, but said, I dare. The minister was hanging
a Japanese scroll in fifteenth century rivers.
He said. "Do you take the worst and make soup?
Do you take the best and escalate?" We said,
"I sweat," said, "Nobody mention death."

My husband with his farmer's almanac heart and
the will of a hundred horsepower lunar calendar.
When we travel life is reduced to nouns: key, clock,
money. Roadmap, shower. When we marry we take the verb.
Cohabit, fight, apologize. Procreate, launder.
Out of the cast iron nuptials into the consummate fire.

## Over and Over

Marriage isn't a vessel
it's salt pouring freely
from a clear shaker.
It's a row of blue birds
on a cedar fence.
Suddenly, they lift.
Marriage is a great big AHA!
You sneeze and I say
"Gesundheit."
We waltz Sunday morning
and the weekdays behave.

Musical as cowbells in Sardinia
we married each other twice.
Once for the girl I used to be,
once for the one I would become.
All the time there were uncles dancing.
There was a party going on

a festival of lips.

The mountain is cool and distant
while you, love, claimed me twice.
Once for the man already inside.
Once for the place I made for you,
a silk garment, bits of wool.

What a chance you take
marrying me. I'm a genius
at forgetting names.
Will you become my Rolodex?
I turn over and over all night
but you are perfectly free
to love me, flawed as I am,
to adore my tangled excuses.

I'll give you parrots of light.
I'll tattoo the seven chakras on my body
so you'll know where I'm coming from.
I'll buy you a bicycle, paint it white
and tie macaw feathers on the handlebars.
I'll climb ladders.
I'll change my socks
to ones with silver threads
for dream walking.
I'll even change my way
of eating soup.

Flawed as I am,
You are perfectly free to love me.
To grow old next to my purple grapes sweater,
to entertain my relatives with jokes
about rivers.

In summer when we sleep less
imagine more, the marriage nights fill
all the salt shakers in all the restaurants
of the world. A miracle, don't you think?
And all the waiters and waitresses
of the world, go in next morning and say,
AHA, there's love out there
a steady stream.

In flu season, we wake up
feeling mean. A zipper catches,
toothache, all the prison riots
take place inside our house.
Selfish winds blow through
our pretty windchimes.
The goldfish dies and we
don't even know love.

Then in slow parabolas,
after you've been skiing
and color returns to your lips,
you walk from the car
into feeling again,
down from the high place of the brain
into the heart
that knows fur and skin.
In the lovely brief light
of beeswax candles
we are married over and over.

## Cross Country

The first place was a left hand turn
full of opposition, forbidden in the center
of the city. Chicago found us each sleeping
next to another. Madness, a blond man
with such short hair. You, dozing
by larger breasts. Love then was a stranger
trying to break in. The front door
had a dead bolt lock.

Two days into the country I was loving you.
Your youngest sister followed us into the hay mow
reciting the names of women. It was Wisconsin
she called it courting and spooning.
Below us cows were waiting
for you to toss down alfalfa.
There was a wagon train in your voice
when you asked that we move west.

Marriage became a road map
a California we would fold and unfold
in our lap, tape at the creases
a manageable scale, ten miles to one inch.
Some mornings all I can think of
is iced tea and rest stops.
There's no choice but to drive through
mirages, low oceans of heat.

Honeymoon in Oregon.
You jumped into a river, swept down,
while I watched your swift swimming
back to the bank's tangle.

Walk back to me today, naked through
the willows of the sleeping campground.

## *Not King David*

We left Chicago in my Volkswagen,
all our belongings stuffed in the trunk.
I stopped at gas stations, filled it with regular.
You never talked to me across Nebraska.

By the Platte River, I made you cry.
In a night of mosquitos I badgered you.
Asked, "Do you love me, love me?"
I buzzed you all night till you broke.
We found each other in sleeping bags
lined with red geese flying west.

The hostel at Berkeley was a place
once used by jockeys, those small light men
who love the backs of animals and flight.
A stink bug crawled across my arm.
We fought, you slapped me in the face
and I cried myself to sleep beside the Bay.

The year between was condensed milk,
thick and sweet, it spanned our cultures.
Golden Gate Bridge, Embarcadero, Presidio.
We forged our holy land, white spire and cathedral.
Again, that hand came at me like an omen.
I took that omen home. I married it.

I married, married, married,
in a Mexican wedding dress,
with carnations held in a clutch.
My father pulled me into the bathroom
before the service, "He'll want
the children Catholic."

You sweated into an old sport's coat
with no necktie. I held my hand on your back
against your shirt. I had my ring on.
"He's a good man," my cousin called to say.
"So what if he's not King David."
At that point it was anybody's bible.

## Wisconsin Blue Willow

You could buy a Mercedes and trade it
for that hillside.
A French painting is worth lots more,
but we still dream it,
our first year stretched like canvas
with just the impression of a silo,
maybe three lines and a cow's muzzle.

A moo, it's foggy
and the foghorns of San Francisco
reach us on that waking hillside.
We'd sit over oatmeal
after milking, stare
out the window and you'd say
there's no view like ours

and the train was on cue,
the grooved mystery, a track runner
who panted his way across the valley
below a green crotch of pines.
We'd put our spoons down,
stand in the doorway.

Who goes down to the spring,
listens to the consensus of the watercress?

I'll spend my days carrying
a Wisconsin hillside
on a large platter, blue willow
and the woods below our house,
the pumphouse and the barn,
heifers, our horse, and a chicken pecks
at the pattern near the edges.

We left. We should have bought it.
Your grandma's rhubarb is in a pie
on the plate of strangers.
They sold that raspberry hillside
for a song, for less than singing.

## Reading in Bed

Summer closes like a pink snapdragon.
On my birthday with new coral earrings
we lie across the mattress
each turning
our own pages.

Amazonian jungle in your hands
and my Japanese novella,
implicit as a plate of raw fish.
I stroke you as I read
turn and sleep.

I wake in a tea ceremony,
a vessel you handle with decorum.
Water and whisk, there is history,
the scent of green tea
and not a word.

A page turns once
on the corner of the bed.
In folds, in a heap,
I am that floral orange kimono.

## Dawning on Your Birthday

Your thirty-fifth birthday
and I can't express my love.
My cakes tend to cave in.
My gifts magically transmogrify
into groceries we have eaten.

Our sky had been running to pinks
and purples, the extravagant
colors of Hawaiian shirts.

Ten years we have slept like spoons,
waking 3,000 mornings to your yawn.
I have taken vows. The faded cloth
the sky makes now.

## Back Road to Trout Lake

If we weren't having so much fun
envying the gamble oaks their color,
still vaguely red, we could be miserable,
it is so cold.

Parked in a woods, gloomy at dusk
we played dominoes, you kept score.
Packed all four, in our camper
from the fifties with turquoise Formica
that bacon smell.

Asleep on a bed that converts
from a table, you woke laughing
hysterical with violins.

We hugged, rocking the Coleman lantern
where it hung. The shocks
on the Chevy were no match for us.
You asked what I like and I said, Noise.
So many years loving around sleeping children.

We felt what we hadn't in months
waking to October snow.
I became your love, your lone pine woman
the design in a curve on a pottery bowl.

The stars, the smell of lanterns,
our love of air and two children
breathing their separate dreams,
fogging the camper windows.

In three days there is no time to quarrel.
The snow is fragile on the trees.
The white mantle of the lantern
can crumble with the slightest jar.

## After Making Love

After many days the rains fell
and after angers. The tears-of-feeling rain
a heat-me-up, moose-in-rut,
left-handed-lover-in-diamond-ring rain.

You melted out of the worried dinnertime.
Changed into soft shoes, full beard
traded your currency for coin. I'm a new car,
You cruised me.

Rented an enormous lover's heart
remodeled it for leisure, a Japanese love motel.
All the penises were there
and all the folded ladies.

The Peacemaker was playing
a violin of horse and cat and wood
and I was on the edge of my seat
waiting for the bridge of peace.

The Golden Gate across a lost Brazilian river
painted orange for life. All the species came, the
trees, the beasts of burden and the lamb.
Deep salmon was served up on a black plate.

In ordinary air you tuned me.
Divine breath breathed me.
Your left leg trailed off the bed.
I wrote and wrote the sacred music.

I wrote you down ecstatic
and in bed our perfect. I wrote you
a testimonial speech for the banquet
and gave you seven gold watches

all with my hands.
I put you in time again
out of the delirious
into the lyric.

## *Why People Marry*

People marry to find earth.
They buy a ticket to pain and God.
They buy a house and a pig and stop smoking.
They marry so that their ears
will have something to hear, their eyes
will learn tears. People marry and then grow
feathers for dusting each other's corners.
Roses have thorns. Apples have seeds. Marriages
have refrigerators and perplexities.
If I were a saint I'd stay single
and plant hundreds and hundreds of pines.

*PART II*

# The Middles

## The Middles

In the middle of a life
in the middle of a marriage
shards of glass and grasses
with purple edges,
the heart grows.
In the leisure of winter
in the lessons of summer
days hang limp like clotheslines.
Days hang with children and housework.
Days fasten themselves to breezes
and forget name and place.

In the middle of a life
in the middle of a marriage
the heart grows grave and troubled
but large. It expands with fragrant
quiet love, the woodsmoke love,
the bloodstone love. In the middle
of October, in the middle of autumn
a man stands below raking vines.
A woman is dividing iris
and thinking the span of flowers
and thinking a book she read
where a woman had cancer
and measured life by rhizomes,
each spring was a bonus.

In the middle of a war
in the middle of a peace
the heart grows.
As the mind thins and chills
as the mind empties of names
like a reservoir in the fall
the mind fills with leaf and fish
and reflections of bare elms.
The heart grows deep like a well
like the place you lived
when you first left home.

In the middle of silence
in the middle of the snow,
the heart grows and that's all
it cares to do. Instead of doubt,
instead of tighten and contract,
the heart like a beef cow
the heart like a flock of poultry
grows full of the place and smell
and papers of a marriage.

You write your generous will.
You give testimony to God.
You praise and stop blaming
once and for all. Prayers.
Laughter. You simply retire
like a couple of farm animals.
Like pensions and policies,
touch and fresh apples.
You collect interest that grows
only in the heart.

## Birch Bark Canoes

I'm wild for your skin
for your wild smell
engraves me like a locket.
Open me up, I hold you then and now.
I'm lonely for your arm
as it was, dusty farm
in Wisconsin fixing fence
lean me back against the tug of wire.

We carried all our water
from the pump house rimmed in mint,
slept downstairs under the blue quilt.
A cookstove burned ceremoniously
and in summer, enormous flies congealed
on the screen a dance of the insane.
I was wild for your body
with its long Boy Scout legs.

Just by loving we made phones ring
cars arrive. We read to each other
from Scott Nearing, Euell Gibbons
and Thoreau. We agreed.
Sometimes you called me rich girl,
Jew. There were rumors in town
about my black hair. Sometimes I hated
the farmer taking you over.

You became numb as rutabagas
dark as black radish.
I was wild to be a wife beside you
with canned goods, garlic braids.
You brought a calf into the house,
twenty below, ears frozen back.
You blew into his nose till lungs held
their own. We both cheered

as he wobbled across bird's eye maple.
His hoofs still gelatin left globules.
He sucked my fingers with his warm,
strong mouth, stared from his black wild eye.
I'm wild for the past. Wild raspberries.
For the horse we owned, for the I Ching
we used to name him. I'm resting now,
mid-life calm, the hurricane's dead center,

beside a man dreaming of birch bark canoes
of the north woods, no see 'ems,
sleeping with wide open windows.

# Angry Night

## I. A Body of Heat

Coming up from the garden
where cool air pools
and mosquitos hover, soaker hoses
approximate oasis. Coming up
to the hot body of the house,
wooden and huge, trapped as a rib cage,
the day's piping heart.

The windows are hung with Mexican fabric,
the dishwasher running on rinse. Coming
into the house you built, washing paint
off your arms after a day so many degrees.
I slept late, woke mean. You hammered.
You never stopped, an engine,
inhuman and full of fuel.

Upstairs, I prop a window fan,
it's makeshift here. The fan runs
like a maniac, its windmill arms
wave, "Too hot, too hot!" I'm grouchy
as broiled meat, as tender as blisters
from hot fat. I'm smack in the anger century
with its costumes of sweat and vocabulary of curse.

I have a deficiency of Vitamin A. Your hand moves
with its audacity, I scream, "Fuck off hand,"
though not with my mouth, a window closed on heat.
I roll to the edge of the bed and you come calling.
You pursue like the Humane Society
the rabid dog. Goodwill Industries,
the Salvation Army, you work your conversion.

You move up onto me like you mean business.
I am the bank, you're certain I'll give a loan.
You come through me like purslane takes over
the garden, a wild determined weed,
the one Gandhi ate and he loved peace.
You grow over me like the succulent purslane,
because that's what my closed eyes provide.

The ocean of fan,
an upper floor apartment
somewhere in the past with paper blinds.
You, a stranger,
nothing but a stranger
and the night in its heat
giving me off like sudden breath.

## II.  Love's Neighborhood

I know everything about bedrooms
in heat, the slow whir of love.
You thought I'd say fans,
for you can hear fans turn
in the background, always,
of summer night,
but I mean, love turns.

It's been a long time the same bed,
the same man. I'm the devotee
of love's resurrection from the dead.
I pray in the face of divorces, in the dumb
face of anger, I turn to my audacious faith.
My precepts are: nothing is perfect,
expect less, rejoice when able.

Last night a man I barely knew came onto me.
I gave up on a hundred religions,
I gave words back to all the therapists.
I wanted to take up Akido at 1 a.m.
He was the culprit behind the heat,
the bum who set the barometer,
that villain, that blamed one, bad weather.

The house was an alien body of torpor
with this cat burglar, this looter.
But remember those fan blades turning air
when they move become invisible.
He did too, turned into a stranger
with no past, only love's pure intention.
I caught that whiff, an old barroom smell.

I became, again, love's expert
in love's best neighborhood.

# And Dream Is Quilt Is Comforter

## I.

Children hide teeth under pillows
in wads of Kleenex, in fists.
A wife runs to the clothesline
takes off sheets full of wind
in the sprinkles before storm.
She plods upstairs to make the grown son's bed.
It is summer with sleep coming on.

Cities light automatically.
Cash slips through the fingers
of a man with slick hair.
His date wonders how long
till the money's gone
they are dancing.
She, with permed hair
and a skirtlength that matters.
Dancing, after all day standing
shampooing the white hair with bluing,
the auburn. They don't converse
until the brief drive home.

It is danger time to drive.
Bats come out. The owl lingers
dives at a prairie dog.
In diners Bun-o-matics drip.
Waitresses drop quarter tips into aprons
bus boys haul greasy tubs
through swinging doors
careful not to annoy the cook.
It is somewhere between seven and ten
everywhere in the states
and things are just getting started.

## II.

Eyelids are closed now, sleep is thickening.
Parents slide quarters under pillows
and children turn their heads
shift their torsos and breathe heavily two breaths.
A wife stares into the back of a sleeping man.
She knows every scar, her eyes may wake him.

And in the city
beneath invisible shooting stars
the slick haired man is talking quickly
and she is wondering when will it ever end
the flattery, the unbuttoning
that finishes the evening.
A new breath and waiting for anger
the key turns harshly in the ignition.

The four boys whose mother works nights
are counting meteors.
The shift changes in hospitals.
No one enters the truck stop for one hour.
A counter is wiped, the curved lines dry.
Everyone sits. The oldest waitress
unlaces her white crepe-soled shoes.
Babies who choose to be born now
are loved just as much by mothers.
It is deep in the night.

## III.

Dreams form and eyelids flicker.
Many tonight will dream of fishes, but few remember.
The husband and wife who recall
will be amazed and compare fish dreams.
Their marriage is blessed
and will last a hundred years.
A six-year-old will wet the bed
and a tired mother forget the lost tooth
of her youngest who still believes.

Under the Lone Star quilt a man dreams of flying.
The whole Ohio town has flying dreams
in a silent sky with slight moist breezes.
Some will miss their planes
and others spread their arms to aerial views
of farms, avenues with oak trees
buckeyes forming inside green spikes.
One child dreams her heart is a shining buckeye.

The Bear Paw quilt lies above a woman
in the rented resort cabin.
Its weight smothers her. The next bed looks lighter
a pine tree pieced in green and white.
She can't sleep and thinks of quilters
the fingers of women working together.
They borrowed names from dreams
the Drunkard's Path, King's Crown, Wild Geese Flying.

## IV.

Alarm clocks go off in homes of the unfortunate
who lose their dreams
swear as they drive to work.
Millions of pairs of glasses
are taken from nightstands
slipped on the nose.
Children grab up their pillows
and some are awed by silver.

The slick haired man is alone.
Sleeping, he has grown disheveled.
His thoughts turn to coffee and aspirin.
A wife hugs her husbands back
optimistic at dawn.
The moon floats over the clothesline.
A piano player can't restrain herself.
Risking the complaints of neighbors
she fingers the keys
begins the day with Haydn.

## After Reading Love Lyrics From India

Loving summer night.
The gnats bite, the
insinuations of mosquitos.
Box elder bugs striped, black
yellow and black on the wall.
We peel off the heat
in layers, we have to talk.
Strip down, insignificant
as bug nonsense.
Late, we get down to business
and turn the light sheets of summer
into tents, where a dark Hindu
lady lies down on top
of the blue god.

## *Florida Vacation*

Last night it stormed.
We woke in our efficiency apartment
two blocks from the ocean. We loved
better than in ages, so good
it shocked you. We always do
startle each other. That's why
we last so long. Certain lovers.
We know how to amaze love.
Just when we thought it was dead,
we cry, "Easter Sunday!" and the body
is gone from the tomb.

## Snow Storm

Once I drove in a snowstorm
colored by red salt, all the highway
from New York to Boston, sobbing.

Now I stay home for love.
I put another log on, I thaw meat.
I gather in the wash when the snow starts.

Hope and I play chess, I fight
with the teenagers about housework,
all on account of the bank of love

that you and I founded. Romantic, the critics
whisper in the wings. If you saw this place
with its clutter and Catholic candles,

with its board games and scatter of books.
With its down again snow outside
and the white horse and the brown,

you'd know that this isn't a life,
it's the dream of a life being lived
by regular lovers, with a blessing here

and a curse there. With an evil eye watching
and the whole family knocking
on wood.

*PART III*

# The Russian Room

## Icons

By the zoo in Central Park
a couple sits in Europe. He reads.
He wears a hat and beard,
Jewish as I am,
Russian like you.

She in a white flat hat.
Her feet in small heeled shoes point in.
Her skirt has pleats, she fidgets
as if she's pregnant
but she's not.

All the while the man
leans into his book, hand over his mouth,
telling her implicitly, silence, wife.
This is his signal, my dear one
my little mandlebrot, my queen.

She has a black and yellow shirt,
checkered bright as a taxi. She lifts
her left foot out of the black shoe.
She rests her head on her fist.
Darkly he reads on.

In the Ramble the trees bloom.
Lovers kiss up at Belvedere Tower,
and the polar bear nudges his great body
onto the rocks. I hear the word "mensch"
as he leaves the water.

It drizzles.
At noon the Delacourte Clock plays
"Three Blind Mice" and the animals revolve.
All of them play instruments, the elephant,
an accordion, the goat, a flute.

A snowy owl cranks her pure head
and a man reads a holy book.
His wife, in a flat white hat
twirls her stockinged foot
around and around and around.

## Pavilion

The jazz band played
on a pavilion. Couples danced
close to the unlit edge.
I was admiring the piano player's shoes
black and shiny. You walked in
right out of the fifties and I said,
not missing a beat, Hi Lover.

You once said when we're forty-five
we'll meet, compare divorces.
You never married, I did,
up to the chin in family.
I can still laugh at how I loved you
when we were twenty.
We didn't ride that elevator
up and back a hundred times,
we just dreamed around the edges
of the dark.

I kept everything I ever got from you,
poems from the Japanese, notes
hidden in textbooks,
I kept how it was I loved you.
It's that kind of love I've read in books,
a Russian novel, an old country,
a man and woman aging far apart,
trains run between them daily
but they never ride.

## The Homeless

All night, since I can't escape into your bed
and play in the adult leagues
where the man with perfect pitch
and the most foolish woman of the twentieth century
reunite and copulate a population of lovers,

that dark militia with their uniform of hands
reach into my sleep and beg hours,
with their unwashed fingers, undress me.
They say, "A hot meal. Spare change."
They say, "Please tuck me in."

Every block has life embarrassing itself.
Asleep on the streets on cardboard,
the army of our poor. A part inside
can't hide anymore, climbs out to beg
with paper cups from what is rich.

Just because we don't make love
it doesn't go away. Your hands
weighted on top of the table.
I say, with my fingers, "A hot meal."
Washed in all my parts, "Please tuck me in."

I leave town tomorrow.
Again on Thursday night, the homeless,
awake with their eyes
no one will meet, stares
that evaporate stars.

This new Calcutta
where we won't touch.
We clutch what we own to our centers.
The homeless reside on their fingers
next to cement.

## *The Lover*

I don't have a lover
but I have an old guitar.
I can't play it and nobody
can tune it. Instruments
shrink in the southwest
because of dry air,
so much sun.

I never had an outside lover.
I say, "Honey." I say to myself,
"Sweetie." I can call myself
these tender terms. That's not the way
God played you on this earth, this time.
You good, good wife. Just sweet Jesus
and you ever were so clean.

## Dark Train Pulling

You, I haven't seen since the turn of the century.
There was a train then, always about to depart.
Or a letter traveling across Europe by rail.
A boat full of people who all looked forward
towards a better life of tailor shops and diamonds,
away from the small villages of Estonia.

In the old country, you lived in Hungary
but you weren't Hungarian. Russia,
but you weren't Russian. You were only a Jew
and not allowed to purchase land.
I want you like my people wanted soil.
That was the trick, my wanting and your no.

Denial works to wed a past to longing.
And now, like a promised land, you arrive.
Startling horizon, your suitcase,
something foreign stamped on the side.
A message I've needed all my life,
"Lose everything," it says, "you know how."

You arrived from the other country,
the past, dark train pulling, sparks over coal.
At death there's another tunnel, I've heard.
Of all the faces and the bright light,
yours will still beckon towards a bliss.
My dark hair, your dark hair, an America.

# The Russian Room

I've spent the day among photos,
I'm that calm. All day
you aren't my husband
but I hear your music.
I saw the red embroidery
from Hungary hang on the wall
of our mutual friend.

Now I ride the peaceful train south,
Mt. Kisco, Chappaqua, Valhalla.
I'm so tired, I want your shoulder.
The man across the aisle
studies osmosis, that lucky voyage,
while I feel New York on me like a suntan.

I was playing Risk-All,
that open-mouthed game adults try.
A Russian roulette without bullets,
just you and me in the Russian Room
full of water glasses and napkins.

Adultery is a word with perfect pitch,
has inside it sultry and the necessary pain.
The heart, I hear, has more room than blood.
After a lover, there's a wet scent
that I never fail to know.

It's Grand Central, time to gather
up my things. Outside it rains.
I hail a taxi, ride it right through
my money like I'm sane. I call you up
while my clothes are still wet.

There's not much to say.
I run my finger around a wine glass
to make her sing. I take my place
in the album beside you, want to be
in black and white on the last page.

# Brevity

The great and frightening thing
about being adults is that
by now we know
we can't save each other.

I came to you out of long-term marriage,
institutionalized, but great benefits and views.
And you from solitude, that study you've made,
New York libraries, jazz festivals, the road.

Over sushi we were delicate, gave our best,
told stories of men and women
in condensed detail, more entertaining
than anything on Broadway.

The next night, this time Italian,
I almost strangled on arugula
laughing and leaning against the wall
at our ridiculous and certain lives apart.

Then I cried, drunk on very little wine.
I offered money for your body, all my cash.
I quoted Zorba the Greek on women's invitations to bed
and watched the waitress who knew you well watch me.

We got out of there, walked towards midtown.
The marquee as we kissed goodbye
lit the already lit 87th and Broadway,
"Women on the Edge of a Nervous Breakdown" showing.

And you, with your immaculate kind hand,
left me there to my own beauty,
that place you took me sightseeing.
A brief holiday. Then you
back to your life of music and notebooks, me,
into the rough and verdant garden of family love.

## Night Words

At the wedding I drink champagne
along with the bride and groom.
At the funeral I drink other things.
But in the night, when I'm alone

with neither the bride, the groom
nor all my ancestors watching from picture frames,
I put on my own black jacket and my favorite hat
and I go down alone and open the door

where poetry comes out. Nobody you know,
but I know every face, all the women
are sweet, like singers at a wedding.
All the uncles lean over, take my hand.

Late at night is where the stories are.
They live in the dark with their own glow.
None of this is about roosters or gold.
Nothing of forests and huts on chicken's legs.

It is about the night which is my only mind.
About a coat, a hat, and a house,
all the relatives and women with sweet voices
and strong hands. It is about the impulse to do good.

It is about each person I ever held on to
and some who let themselves out secretly.
It is as much about a mirror, sorry to admit,
as it is about no visions and no image.

Just a plain black jacket for the middle of the night
and a wide brim hat to keep off indoor weather
and all the books who are my only family.
After all is said. After all is done.

# PART IV

# Reaching Across

## Family as Still Life

At the table of who knows when
a family is stopped for a framed moment.
The son becomes still and sad-eyed, his mind whirs
invisible bicycles. Tires spin inside him,
momentum of summers, learning to swim.

The girl under faint make-up,
radiates light, the family chandelier.
She has the fullest glass of water,
the wet future poised in her body:
pastel, gouache, charcoal.

The baby, fat darling of bibs, caught mid-hiccup,
she jumps a bit. She's three dimensions of rose,
peachs and apricot jams, she is the honeycomb.
At late harvest the light stretches
sweetly you smell death in the leaves.

The parents are a pair, a mom and pop
pas de deux. Their anger evaporates in silence.
Their old passions woven and solid, a worn tablecloth
damask and blue. Their eyes say, Voilá!
Examine their furnishings, menus.

The husband thinks: Bali, Sumatra, scuba. The wife:
horticulture, lover. No domestic arrives
to clear, but the light comes up, the daughter
grumbles to her feet. Introduce noise,
all life breaks loose.

The chord is spinal, umbilical, and major.
Dessert is served with five voices,
a harmony of need. Pass the love,
more kindness, save me some generosity.

### You Are Forty Years Old at the End of the Twentieth Century. What Will You Do When Love Comes?

When Love comes your car radio will glow blue
and the country western songs will be faithful.
You will love your old husband with abandon,
even the way he chews will fascinate.

When Love comes you will paste an amulet
on all the foreheads of New York City
that says, Love, turn down
the corners of my bed but not my mouth.
Sacrifice your lips but not the land.
Make me whole, take me whole, make me holy.

When Love comes your children will be educated
because no one will run out of patience.
You will hold an election where passion and ecology
win. You will swoon with your love of vegetation,
the broccoli, the piñon, the sweet honeydew.

When Love comes riding a Gamaloops,
Dr. Seuss will be your family physician.
I can't tell you how happy you'll be
but I know I will be gladder than kites,
I'll be childlike under Bo tree,
under olive, more miraculous than lion and lamb.

When Love comes, let me warn you,
it will take a heart breathed full.
The heart the Indians grew hunting deer in the woods.
It will take the heart the porpoises have for underwater love.
It will take the heart of the cliff swallow, that light.

Prepare yourself. Grow hands
big enough to stay bombs.
Hands sweet enough not to bruise forests.
Great Love will soft shoe in,
in tap shoes of silver, will woo you,
croon to you, and not even money,
will be as seductive as love.

## Breakfast with John and Michael

The rooster knows flamenco.
The face of my first lover is soft, I want to taste it.
At this rate, we will be sixty when next we meet,
instead of gray, we will be whitening.

The face of my past lover is close, the eggs are scrambled.
I will not get in the New Yorker for saying this.
Instead of gray and nervous, we will be white
and leavening into a life of bone.

I will not get in the New Yorker for saying this.
The face of my husband knows flamenco, his eyebrows
lift above a world of politics and bones.
I drink from Frida Kahlo, blood and paint

and the face of my once lover, his eyebrows quirky,
strips me down to bone like cactus after.
I drink from Frida Kahlo, blood and pain
and beer from Mexico, the lone stark wives.

Strip me down like blouses in the sixties.
I am engulfed by children and young chickens
and beer from Mexico, the lone stark life alone,
because we chose this place far out of town.

I am engulfed by children and two pasts.
I give myself over and over to men like Sabbath.
I chose this place, far from the New Yorker.
We live the holy family, roses and Jesus and Sundays.

I give myself over and over to dishes like rosaries.
Chickens walk across my porch like Central Park.
I chose this family, roses and Sundays,
a centerpiece of paper flowers, my former lover, formal.

Children walk across my porch like Central Park.
I concentrate on Michael, lanky and freshly shaven.
A still life of paper flowers, classic like a husband.
My thighs are big and wine spills out of marriage.

I concentrate on John, heavier, freshly shaven.
Soon our friends get married at the town hall in Española.
My thighs are big, champagne will fill the goblets.
How many brides and grooms stand at this moment?

Soon our friends get married at the town hall.
John and Michael sit like cronies, drink their coffee.
How many brides and grooms stand gray as pewter?
Next time we meet, we will be sixty, we will be wine.

## Triolet a Trois

I'm cleaning house for Victor Hernandez-Cruz.
Don't ask me why, he's not even my type,
back in Puerto Rico with his white suit.
I sing, cleaning house for Victor Hernandez-Cruz,
a man who drinks with his hands the world's blues.
Some male poets fill my ears with hype,
but I'm cleaning house for Victor Hernandez-Cruz.
Don't ask why. Invent it as I type.

Sometimes to clean you have to have a lover,
a man walking out the screen door into lilac,
down into the garden, through the arbor
in a white suit. Any man cleans into a lover.
He says, your husband knows you well, you're clever.
Beyond romance I'm known in common fact.
Sometimes you clean your old house, take a lover,
fill vases with dreamtime or a man outdoors in lilacs.

Flowers are swollen, the night's a balm.
Nobody home, my music soft, the polyphonic bullfrog night
reminds me of Puerto Rico, or New York, jazz clubs. Calm
as flowers swollen, the night's a balm.
The man walks away, removes his white suit from my arms.
Marriage is anti-aphrodisiacal, it causes flight.
The flowers are swollen, no night's a balm,
everybody home, the music blasting, the bullfrog night.

## Conversations in Blue

*(after the painting by Henri Matisse)*

Matisse said, darling.
This painting of me in my striped pajamas
And you in your dressing gown
Is not about us.
It's not that you sit on your chair
And I face you standing
Flanked by the flat blue wall between.

Conversations in blue,
A background against which we quarreled,
We dined. Amelie, Henri Matisse said,
This is about Monmartre, blue eye shadow
On ladies of the night. Blue rings of light
Around streetlamps, the sky
on extraordinary mornings.

It's about blue.
The way I hear America described,
Great open vistas and plains.
It's chicory on roadsides in Provence,
Bottles of tonic on a windowsill,
Night eyes on a deaf tomcat
Who fights for his gray life.

Amelie, the painter said,
Turning to look not at her
But at blue, this is not about us.
Not our hands on each other
Or the fresh fresh space between desires.
Not about form, your hair loose,
Piled up, or swept by a blue wind.

My dear, my sweet, her husband said,
His eyes now closed though yet he stood,
This is about the color blue.
You and I are merely bodies.
We love then we exit on cue.
This is my eternal life,
The color blue.

## *To Dusk*

I used to pound the streets in tears wondering
if I were French. Of if the squirrels understood.

Then I moved around, circumnavigating the world
of the disenchanted. Magellan finally made sense.

Cardamon, hemp, and clove. A Hindu caste mark.
How did I get to this room, slowly, and slower

I traveled in your arms. A flannel voyage.
Concurrence of obstinancy and rejoicing.

I learned that sentiment has a head and a heart.
Chinese women kill their husbands by excessive courtesy.

That shocked me. Took me back to you who I want
to live forever. I vow to be honest and uncivil.

I told a man I hardly knew, a newlywed, "We have
an Italian marriage." He was Italian, began to cry.

You were so beautiful on the phone. Delicate
about the most pernicious things. Taxes. Insurance.

Your voice said not to worry. Not so heavy. Sweetness
clear from Phoenix. Years develop and tones become revealed.

Last night I rented movies, rocked in your grandmother's
chair. I was so lonely I called my mother. Monumental azaleas.

Calamitous flowers. My mother and I do best by distance.
You and I also. My children I carry under my shirt.

Laughter in the morning. Tears by nightfall. Halloo
is the entry above hallow in my Webster's. Dusk is a verb.

## Two Cars Cruising on Two Saturday Nights

Marriage looms like immense foreplay for death.
I drove fifty miles in the wrong direction, want you.
You offer space, think I want vistas more than your
head in my lap, anywhere on me, your personal skull.

On that acid trip in San Francisco, another Saturday,
we rushed to City Lights Books, old Beat slice of pie.
I had a date with a mustached man who played guitar.
You drove me there like the Eskimo's shared wife.

I was still flashing from the drug of you, stepped
from our car into an older model, drove away
over the Bay Bridge. The sunset, jealousy free,
was Hare Krishna yellow. You went home alone.

The musician's mouth tasted of me and curry,
while you were the mouth of flowers. I hadn't married,
didn't know how long this will you-won't you might last.
It's the Haight, the flavor burned out and saddened.

Tonight I cruise in a red Subaru. It's rainy, Saturday
in June. I'm so alone, Jesus at the corner church
in stained glass lit from a light inside, looks sexy.
Jupiter, Venus, and Mars triangulate above.

I'm all three Marys. I drive past two nostalgias,
motorcycles leaned against the drive-in liquor.
Two long-haired men squat. Forget the Sixties,
I want a western. Your hot body tapping mine.

Spurs, horseback, and an oasis called SEX,
an expensive hotel. I light the VACANCY sign.
I'm prowling the Nineties for the man who said back then,
"Be true. Never swap horses in the middle of a stream."

We've been the same river cutting a valley.
Ride hard. Don't trade love.

# *The Angel of Marriage*

Utterly alone
the angel of marriage longs for union.
It matches people up by mistake
in its blind drive to pair.

Not the wisest of angels,
but the most loving. A cross
between the forgiveness angel
and the angel of longing, odd Baroque hybrid.

Classical music
plays through the angel of marriage.
Wine glasses break under its stomped foot.
Legal documents line its Byzantine garments.

Angel of stress
and dishes, angel of rice. Teapot angel,
angel of folded laundry. Beautiful, loyal angel
of small town husband, big city wife.

Mercurial angel
of form change and myriad days. Right out
of the Bible, angel of long haul. You, with your needle
for darning, your fervent epoxy of sex.

Hover above us.
Help do the work that piles up in loads.
Give us Sundays of psalms. Do childcare. Be faithful.
Rescue the holy from the matrimony.

## Holy Matrimony Sestina
*written during the Gulf War*

It is the fifth week of the war.
My children eat for dinner, history.
My list of groceries limited to candles
because peace is blue and lit by a match.
It took us weeks to come again to sex.
I became each evening every soldier's wife.

You ask me how it is to be a wife.
I answer, it's momentous, peace and war
between us, but the ultimate dissolve is sex.
Anyone on fire by peaceful flanks makes history,
anyone with sparks makes my best match.
Flint of anger, balm of tear and candle.

At night by Virgin of Guadalupe candle
I look into the dark for what is wife,
what is husband. We're elaborately matched.
Your scant impression of the day is war,
night's challenge is to alter history
and the medicine for holy war is holy sex.

We did not become famous for sex,
that's a story told by a stranger's candle.
But I'm always willing to make history,
become the woman who brought an altar to wife.
My husband said, I don't want to be at war.
Treat me like anybody else. We match.

We're rough. Less polite than when we made the match.
Round one, chores. Round two, children. Where's sex?
Somewhere between new moon and untouched by war.
Someplace smelling of pine, someplace called kindle.
I walk into a room, I'm nobody's wife.
Where is that sweet young girl of history?

He asks me, how did we become history?
Our bed already two wars deep. We're matched
by habit and by children, the flowers of sex.
By furniture and dishes, he nicknames me "strife."
Lit by water, lit by bickering. No candles
hold a flame to our double wick. No holy war.

My blessed warrior, inside our history
is the family candle, the kitchen safety match,
the strike anywhere sex of husband and wife.

## Solid as Chocolate

"I want to do with you
what spring does with the cherry trees."
Pablo Neruda
from TWENTY LOVE POEMS

We live together, the thing is
I'm always right. You're always right.
Quirks. You knew it. You came to me,
tiptoed over the sea of poems

on my Chicago basement apartment floor
to my bed on the floor, loved me
in full sight of the typewriter,
it's silent keys already taking notes.

And I use you in poems, and you use me
in jokes. And in bed, in bed, we use
each other, we use each other up,
more rainfalls in our hearts.

And where is your new heart?
Out in the oatfields, out in the barn
milking with your father. Up in the mountains
fishing for the one white trout.

Today I was driving into town, crying. I love you
more than an enemy. I need you more
than city of Chicago needs Lake Michigan.
Don't ever die. Don't ever run off

with whatever other woman loves you more.
She'll be just as impossible as I am
once you get to know her. Valentine.
You prefer horses, Brahma bulls, a fall.

"They're really solid," my friend the therapist
says. Solid as chocolate that melts,
is bad for your skin, expensive,
exploits workers in Mexico.

You're always right. I'm also right.
We live at right angles in a house
of right angles. You built the house,
the love is still under construction.

It can be hot one taken for granted day,
and the next, all the blossoms of Velarde,
New Mexico, the expanse of apple, the orchard
of apricots, all of us, freeze. I say this:
consider the blossom and the fruit and the way
we fight towards love.

## Heron Lake

You chose me and I chose you
a lake as blue as confidence.
Along the shore, what rock there is
is fragments. I stand
on crumbled sandstone.

The more distance, the more fragments.
There is no one truth.
There's the truth my body tells.
It won't lie to you, listen
at the place behind my knees.
That is my weather and the thick length
of me shows, middle age and all,
what's become of me.

I'm standing here alone
on the shore of Heron Lake.
It rains. My children
in a turquoise rowboat
with you at the oars. I'm slipping
away from family to solo admissions.
My lifetime laps out from this spot.

You are in a rowboat
going back and forth
for sheer momentum in this sleepy weekend.
In this economy, arm and water
equal movement. I long for another mind,
Wallace Stevens at Key West.

I have instead the oar's familiar sound,
the same plop and rip in all lakes
of the world. You have a square chin,
solid as the state of Wisconsin.
Even when unhappy with myself
I locate a place in you
where the boat returns,
a lake in the mountains.

Each other, each other,
the oars say.

## Dark Fiesta

Fiesta floats go by on a night highway,
a festive decor of cornstalks and skeletons,
wildflowers and beauties waving.

There's danger in these mountains.
An avalanche buries,
I shovel you out of yourself.

You pinch my nipples. I bite hard.
Driving on black ice,
about to skid, getting from far to near.

I want to unbutton the 300 buttons
that run down the front of your soul.
Strip off the shirt you hide from me in.

Climb down into the basement
so we can make more noise. Sure,
go to the bathroom first. Start empty.

Cats assemble outside our door,
scratch all the way to bare wall.
Your ground is my sky.

Rescue, rescue, it's only one patent cure
that works well for a while
for absolutely everything obdurate and cold.

Talk to me. Open the slot in your face that lipstick
covers. Fling me from myself, my hometown.
Rape my name by saying it too loud.

Change me. Polish my toenails red.
Show me the inside of the out,
the dark faces of love, all the dark harvest.

## Loneliness

Last night at the Japanese hot tub
I had a date with a man I knew too well,
the way I know sugar, black tea, or salt.
I had a date that felt like corduroy
and I sang Rumi quatrains, the stars, absolute.

Steam from the bath fogged both our glasses
but we kept them on and the ache of shadow
crossed your body. Mine was a moon past full.
I sang about a drunkard, you took it
to mean beer, when all the time it was God.

I was so tired from hot water, began
to explode into fatigue and crying. The water
became tears I sang through. I forgot it was called
relaxing, a word I'd lost in California
in a rented apartment when I first lived with you.

You stretched out like an X and I stretched out
like a Y and we floated there and silence
came out as a moon. "Three quarters," you said
and I gave in to the bath of moonlight. We drove
home slowly, so happy or sad I couldn't tell.

I went to bed first and out of my dreams
of chickens your mouth came from nowhere,
all around me the lonely wings of fowl,
I don't know how to write about this marriage.
It's loneliness I want and loneliness you give me

back of my childhood, place I belong
like the city of Pittsburgh. Here we are loving
reduced to our simplest roles, a flat-chested
girl, a skinny boy with arms full of hay,
reaching across after so many years.

## Exile

I like sleeping down here by the fire
where you exiled me, upstairs coughing
and feeding on dark fever. All night you play
music from the fringe of the classical mind.
I hear bass notes through the floor and think
of death, that deep note thumping your chest.

All night I dreamed my car was lost
by the Albuquerque airport. I wandered
past armless men and legless men,
men ground by the city into grimy meat.
I took refuge with a one-armed man,
he lit his cigarette by shooting a gun.

In early light there's hoarfrost on the grasses.
Out the window the horse coughs and you cough
like a smoker, like your father with his milk barn
and pack of Camels. You cough into your manhood,
grow beautiful as a woman in this sickness.
I think your large heart is beginning

its final opening. You will be completely you
by morning. This illness will be the one
to change you. I bring tea of fresh ginger, tell you
this secret tea and angels will be the cure.
I leave the room, you have flung your arms open,
"Michael the Archangel" you say privately, not joking.

Angels hear you, your voice grown
from an altar boy's. After a hundred years
of Catholic schooling, after being so good,
you'll wake lightheaded in a found new country,
and I'll rejoin you in our bed,
our flesh so far from homeless.

## Owl and the Pussycat Pantoum

Come closer, tell me in words how you reclaim me.
I sang you "The Owl and The Pussycat" while we made love.
I am too old and married, the blue fires turn brown.
My milk is so different from your milk.

I sang you the poem, "The Owl and the Pussycat."
I've read that holy people have the best sex.
My milk is no different from your milk.
Not man's from woman's, but city milk and country.

I've heard that older people are very sexy.
God gets involved with loving, the bed's a church.
Not man and woman, but city loving country.
My parents had twin beds, I climbed into the crack.

God gets involved with loving, the bed's cathedral.
I grow old married, the blue fire lasts forever.
My parents had twin beds. I climbed into double flame,
said, "Come closer, tell me in words how you reclaim me."

## The Sugar Orchids

Sometimes in the night he is a beautiful
and mysterious husband. He brings me to orchids.
He ingratiates my thighs with kisses
he never had for any other wife. He takes the knife
out of the day like King Arthur. He's impaled
on the rock of marriage, rescuing each dollar,
fixing each alarm.

His fingers play "Au Claire de Lune."
I'm strummed. He borrows the night for me
from old women in black dresses.
His tongue is not afraid, he licks
the sugar skulls from Mexico.

He invites the clematis to grow up the bedstead
because they need their roots in the dark.
Contradictory vine, their blossoms need sunlight.
If I'd lie, I'd say, their fragrance is grape,
but I'm truthful. They only flower
in sex, as everything tonight
is wearing mystery.

Clematis is married to the trellis, morning
glory to strings up the eastern window,
flagrant blue, opens shameless in daylight.
Daylight astounds me, just how classical daylight
is, a formal arrangement of pain and duty.

I want to live at night now. Send the children
to school, arrange the shutters for noon
to go black. Send the parcel post man
to deliver me from daylight. Night-blooming cereus
is so rare, the women wait up weeks
until it blooms. I'm like that now. I'll poise
here for flowering.

And old women in black dresses pin on a corsage.
They say, "Be young. Be brave and young for us."
I wear their sorrow and their flowers.
He is wiping his mouth now.
Nobody could get any younger,
you couldn't get the sugar orchids any sweeter.

## I Don't Know Wide But I Know Deep

We mated with skin that could be from any century.
There is no tattoo on the body
of the man I love. There is no work
too long or hard for the man I love,
including me with my curious ardor for pain.
He can take dark like anything on earth.

I want to love him till we're bruised.
My arms with a mark of wings,
Tantric art on my shoulder, a symbol
the shape of his teeth.

If he had breasts he'd be my perfect lover,
some extra softness where the heart sounds.
I'm his Parisian, he's my American.
The war could begin any minute. It's urgent.
Let's decorate the instant with sin.

There is no memory in the belly of the man I love.
My head rests there, has rested, will rest,
a conjugation of peace. There is no money
in the pocket of the man I love.
We can have everything, Paris in the Thirties,
small cafés, women dance with women,
men with men, all dressed to kill.

He's naked. He's wearing black,
I'm all in cotton and silks.
Under that part that puts on garments,
deeper than the place which circulates blood,
grows the great spacious face
of the love I love, an arrival
more pressing than winter.

Torch singers, contortionists,
all of us came from this,
this sacred assembly of skin.
Shot full of stars, I enter him.
Something larger and larger takes up the room.
Open the windows, he calls.
Open them.

## Hindu

The husband finds the wife more lovely
than she finds herself. And she sees him
younger than the world. Is this not love?
The other morning her legs framed his face,
a sacred text of sex between them. Too
Kama Sutra, they both came undone
with laughter.

          Outside the window
a perfect waning moon. Plowing her,
a farmer. Framing him, an artist.
In the other the beauty each had a heart
from lacking. Tarnish on silver is found
by some to give a lustre more stirring
than polished sterling. She sang a raga
without knowing, in the tones
that issued forth out of her coming.

## Ardent

It took years to be the faithful wife I always was.
Now I harvest what I find in other people's eyes:
the celibate and the lover, the lonely botanist.

I bring the wanton home condensed and charged.
Men and women look me safe in the eye.
Watch me turn the impossible.

But a face comes into focus slowly. Years later
a middle-aged Krishna chases a full grown
gopi around the bed, each with a waist and a wish.

Each a kiss from another lifetime, where men made
love to all women in one body and women had all
the sweets of the marketplace.

## September Rains

Middle of the night now, it rains.
What was missing all summer condenses and spills.
At the end of peaches, when the swimming pool closes.
The dog smells like she's just been born
out of the mother dog. Thunder. At 3 AM
my three sweets sleeping. My fourth away
at higher education. "Why can't our house
be like a regular house," my eldest innocently
asks? I cry for days at my ineptitude.
To be a mother in the middle of this
reign of chaos. Who made this mess?
The rain is God's. Yom Kipper Eve, sins.
Fasting and letting go. I let the cat out
and she arrives in by mysterious entry.
The dog jingles her tag. The rain breathes
into the mess of this house and blesses:
scent, sound, love, and ineptitude. My family
surrounds me, as God does, ineffable.

## Peaches

The children scream soccer sounds. I face
east through cracked windshield, a car
Spider Woman would drive. The clouds, flotillas
of dark moisture. My birthday passed. One child gone.
The eldest returns to fill our house and watch
how we are now that she is not of us.

The summer ended in peaches. And how
did we get to this, nights French kissed
by loving? Old married becomes too erotic
to speak. The secret within old couple's eyes.
We stumble into the loving terrain. Long term
ache of the turn into ripe after stasis.
Flotillas of peaches in the sink, you peeling
and I filling the fruit jars, handed down
from your mother, adding the syrup, running
the knife around the inside of the jar.

## Post Coital

All day post coital, you reverberate
both man and woman. Even our therapist
says you look handsome. I'll name you
Mr. Tzedakah, which means of good quality.

I'm storing up for winter. There's
always another winter and an Egypt.
Tear out the raspberries, the Pyracantha,
the goat heads, the locust, the rose,

anything with thorns. Last night half
a white moon planted asters, half
a dark moon sobbed. I came from coal dust.
You came from milk. We met in wind from the lake.

Even Kaballah has a place for your leg
a place for my leg, rungs of the same ladder,
branches of the same tree. We were flying up
all night and we were climbing down.

We held hours before action, it was less
Italian and more Viennese, that is to say
waltz and not tarantella. My mother met
your father and flirted. Your mother baked

a pie for my father. All night was a washing
as if the leaves cleansed their hands with rain
before a meal. I only saw you once since morning.
You said my lipstick accentuates chamisa.

Your head is still on my breast. My hand
around you. Throb is a word more autumnal today.
Aspens throb as much as quake. Hearts cha cha.
Seasons migrate like geese or grown children.

If I weren't so happy I'd be forlorn,
like her eyes under the word divorce.
I'll go there with widows and divorcees
and men with AIDS avoiding Fire Island.

The Dalai Lama has never felt this. I have
no system for this loving, except the four
seasons and the four chambers of the heart,
the four emotions: joy, fear, sadness, and pity.

Grace of last light on roadside wildflowers.
Graves at the Jewish cemetery need tending.
My own graven image on your chest, miraculous
shroud where my face stains your shirt.

## Eve Marie's Eyes

I found her in Eden holding an armful of towels.
In my hand I held a silver heart and a fish.
Talked about the eyes that dare to look
brown on brown or hazel on blue.
In her gaze I meet my Absolute.
Told how where I live I avert my eyes,
handsome Spanish man or the native child,
it's cultural, I explain.

Lost in the window
card from my childhood deck.
On its other side I find her very eyes
carved on an ancient mask
so I won't forget.
Eye on eye we meet in a holy land,
without shame or consequence,
to remember why we came.

Saying goodbye and thanking all the time.
Thank bed, thank sandalwood soap, and thanking rain.
I told him yesterday that for five years
I've been learning to give "Thanks" to a compliment.
Now "You're welcome" is my next frame
So, today, facing two deer and my long way home
I heard the world say "You're welcome"
as I thanked, and I recognized why I came.

And I said, "I can't bear it"
at the ferry gate. "I can't bear it"
has been my refrain. From now
I change my song to sound the depth
I can bear it and I bore it
off to my home, a traveler blessed.
My dark eyes allowed the world
and begin to contain.

The eyes of the animals lead me back into yours.
Man or woman, I am each moment's wife.
The bear looking into my eyes from a photograph,
has given me nerve to carve my name in you.
You will never forget me
nor will I lose you.
My heart is God's eye
and recollects why I came.

I bear the world home to our loving.
Matchmaking you with my eyes.
I want to gaze you back to Eden
as I have been Edenized.

## *Why I Love You*

Or you. All comes from down. All
comes from the side of beef we call creation.
All comes from the dark under the bed.
The way death worked me over as a child.

All comes from a dream of wild deer,
or Mary being courted by a voice, all
comes from a man whirling in a century
which disappears and starts glowing.

About singing. About a cloud photographed
by a man who lost his daughter. About promise,
feel light fear in her chest. Win anything
and feel dread. About escaping the Old Country.

Or a because. Possibly, you were there.
Simple. Stark in your leather.
Angle iron in your chin. You were smiling
and mouthed words keyed to my lock.

"I accept," the pain said. First face.
Last. We come and go coded for the common
combination of eyes and lip. Attract to red.
The nude photograph called birthday.

Or action. He puts work before words.
He puts a split log at my feet, feels
expressed. Egg. Budget. He exits. Returns hours later.
And again. Tender engine. We swallow decades.

Or luck. Four directions. Four leaves.
My pocket of talismen. My candles for saints.
Or crossed body parts. Spitting to ward off.
Wearing a necklace of your hair, a ring

set with your tooth. Mezuzah on door.
Kissing. Reciting. Holding the fringe
of prayer shawl in my fingers. Feeling God
is a way of touching wood. Loving

mystery. We could leave it in mist.
Be in a Japanese scroll that is never revealed,
its stream falling, not down, but to center.
Its pines and mountains rolled into each other.

## Rhyme

When blood was pounding in my head
and all our friends unmarrying, you
and I flew here and there, yet kept
the fire from wandering. So far
we've kept the faithful part and now
the death until us part. Our vows
were scant, our vows weren't said
our marriage vows came from your head.
Our marriage vows came from my fear
and rhyming you with me, my dear.
My deer, my dear, my dream, my life.
I've finally become your wife.
I've chosen you as you chose me.
Not heavily or lightly. Not permanently,
not gracefully. But clumsily and stumbling in,
we ended up the next of kin. The rest
is how this moment lies, forever
inside your eyes. You've done for me
I've done for you. Now faithfully,
one becomes two. And two becomes both
one and three, we are the truth's dicotomy.
We married barely slapped from youth.
Now twenty three years in,
fidelity has been my sin.
Husband, we have learned long love.
It's from below as from above.

*Colophon*

Set in PERPETUA & its companion italic :: *Felicity*.
Designed by Eric Gill for Monotype *(1925~30)*.
Built out of craftsman's *flair*
& a rake's *progress*,
each letter stands, roundly or
upright, strong with personality
& merges into a *sprightly* dance
as words form.

◆

*Book design by J. Bryan*

Long time New Mexico Artist-in-Residence, Joan Logghe has
taken her work into the State Penitentiary, The New Mexico School
for the Deaf, Open Hands Art With Elders, the AIDS community,
& schools all over the state. She's been a writing workshop
ringleader from Ghost Ranch *(Abiquiu, New Mexico)* to Hollyhock
*(Cortes Island, British Columbia)*; hostess of the open readings at the
Center for Contemporary Arts in Santa Fe & a hot reader herself
from Talking Gourds Festival to Taos Poetry Circus.
In 1991, she won a National Endowment for the Arts grant for Poetry.
Author of WHAT MAKES A WOMAN BEAUTIFUL *(Pennywhistle)*
& A LUNCH DATE WITH BEAUTY *(Fishdrum)*,
she is based in La Puebla, New Mexico with her husband
& three children in the solar-heated house they built themselves.

◆

*Front cover photograph :: Thayer Carter*
*Back Cover photograph :: Phyllis Boudreaux*